kids' kookiest riddles

Steve Charney

Illustrated by
Rob Collinet

STERLING

New York / London
www.sterlingpublishing.com/kids

This one is for Robin and Caleb

Library of Congress Cataloging-in-Publication Data

Kids' kookiest riddles / [compiled by] Steve Charney; illustrated by Rob Collinet.
  p. cm.
  ISBN 1-4027-2038-6
  1. Riddles, Juvenile. I. Charney, Steve. II. Collinet, Rob.

PN6371.5.K55 2005
818'.60208--dc22

2004028524

Lot #:
10 9 8 7 6 5 4 3 2 1
09/10
Published by Sterling Publishing Co., Inc.
387 Park Avenue South, New York, NY 10016

Distributed in Canada by Sterling Publishing
c/o Canadian Manda Group, 165 Dufferin Street
Toronto, Ontario, Canada M6K 3H6
Distributed in Australia by Capricorn Link (Australia) Pty. Ltd.
P.O. Box 704, Windsor, NSW 2756, Australia

Sterling ISBN 978-1-4027-7850-6

For information about custom editions, special sales, premium and
corporate purchases, please contact Sterling Special Sales
Department at 800-805-5489 or specialsales@sterlingpublishing.com.

Contents

BUGS, BEASTS, AND BIRDS

BIG BEASTS

What animal has the highest intelligence?
A giraffe.

How do you train King Kong?
Hit him with a rolled up newspaper building.

What steps should you take if you see a lion?
Long ones.

What do you get when you cross a tiger with a parrot?
I don't know. But when it talks, you'd better listen.

What's the best way to call a tiger?
Long distance.

I can lift an elephant with one hand.
Can you really?
You find me an elephant with one hand, and I'll lift him.

MARVIN: You can't pull out elephant tusks because they're so tight.
MELVIN: Except in Alabama . . . Tuskaloosa.

TEACHER: Can you give me the names of two bears in the far north?
HARRY: I'm sorry, I don't know any personally.

What do you call a gorilla with a giant stick?
Sir.

What's the difference between a flea and an elephant?
An elephant can have fleas, but a flea can't have elephants.

Do cows give milk?
No, you have to take it from them.

Do you know how long cows should be milked?
The same as short ones.

What two animals do you go to bed with every night?
Your calves!

What do you do when the biggest cow in the world looks you in the eye and says, "Moo."

You'd better moo.

Two cows are in a pasture grazing, and one says, "Moooo."

The other says, "I knew you were going to say that."

FIRST GUY: I used to be a lion tamer. I'd put my right arm inside the mouth of a lion. They called me "Garbanzo the Great."

SECOND GUY: What do they call you now?

FIRST GUY: "Lefty."

FARMER HAYSTACK: Have you ever seen a herd of cows?

HARRY: Sure I've heard of cows.

FARMER HAYSTACK: I don't mean have you heard of cows. I'm talking about a cowherd.

HARRY: What do I care if a cow heard. I haven't said anything she shouldn't hear.

BEASTY BEASTS

How many sheep does it take to make one sweater?
I didn't even know sheep could knit.

TEACHER: Is the kangaroo peculiar to Australia?

HARRY: No, but it sure is to me!

Where do sheep get a haircut?
At the baa-baa shop.

What's a one-eyed deer called?
No ideer.

How come there are no monkeys on the moon?
Because there are no bananas there.

What do you get if you cross a pig and a centipede?
Bacon and legs.

When is the veterinarian the busiest?
When it's raining cats and dogs.

Cats

What happens if you put your cat in the washing machine?
You get a sock in the puss.

What happened to the cat who swallowed a ball of wool?
She had mittens.

Name four animals in the cat family?
The mama cat, the papa cat, and two baby kittens.

HARRY: What's furry, purrs, and is filled with cement?
STEVE: I don't know. What?
HARRY: A cat.
STEVE: What about the cement?
HARRY: I just threw that in to make it hard.

Dogs

Our dog is just like a member of the family.
Which one?

MOE: Why are you so scared of that big dog? Haven't you ever heard the expression, "Barking dogs never bite"?

JOE: Sure, I've heard the expression, and you've heard the expression, but has that big dog ever heard the expression?

What's a sheepdog?
It's an animal you get from mixing sheep and dogs.

What kind of dog would you have if you crossed an Armenian husky and a pit bull?
An Armpit.

What does a dog do on three legs that a man does on two?
Shakes hands.

What does a dog do that a man steps in?
Pants.

CRAZY AUNT DAISY: The last time I saw you, you weren't even a year old, yet you were able to walk.

HARRY: So what? I know a dog who can walk, and he's only six months old.

CRAZY AUNT DAISY: Yes, but he has twice as many legs.

PHIL: I've just come from the board of health. They've concluded that the dog that bit you is mad.

JILL: How do you like that? *He* bit *me,* and *he's* mad?!

How can you stop your dog from barking in the backyard?

Put him in the front yard.

If a dog loses his tail, where would he get another one?

At a retail store.

GUY IN PET SHOP: In this pet shop do you have any dogs going cheap?

OWNER: No, they all go woof.

What has four legs and one arm?
A Pit bull.

HERMAN: Your dog is chasing a man on a bicycle!
SHERMAN: Don't be silly. My dog can't ride a bicycle.

Birds

What's an ostrich?
It's a weird bird that doesn't fly but runs like a horse. Only it runs on two legs, which makes it a pretty weird horse.

What are barn swallows?
They're birds with rather large mouths.

NELLIE: If you pull the string on my parrot's right leg, he sings "America the Beautiful." If you pull the string on his left leg, he sings "Yankee Doodle Dandy."
TELLY: What if you pull the strings on both legs?
NELLIE: He falls off his perch.

What's a peacock?
A chicken in bloom.

Why did the woman cross a hyena with a parrot?
So she could ask him what he was laughing about.

What goes quick-quick?
A duck with hiccups.

Chickens

Where do chickens live when they're in the Arctic?
Eggloos.

How many chickens does it take to screw in a light bulb?
Chickens can't screw in light bulbs, they don't have hands.

When do eggs become runny?
After they hatch into chicks.

What do you get if you put ham in your omelet?
Hamlet.

What do you get if you put chicken in your omelet?
A Chiclet.

Who was Snow White's brother?
Egg White (get the yolk?).

Why did the chicken cross the playground?
To get to the other slide.

Why did the dinosaur cross the road?
Because no chickens were around yet.

Fish

Where do you find the most salmon?
Between the head and the tail.

PROFESSOR: Can fish live out of water?
HARRY: No, they would drown in the air. So actually—
we're even.

What's brown, sweet, and dangerous?
Shark-infested chocolate pudding.

You can tune a guitar, and you can tune a fiddle, but you can't tuna fish—unless it's got scales.

Why didn't the pet shop owner give the goldfish fresh water?
Because it didn't drink what he gave it yesterday.

HARRY: What hangs on a wall, is green, wet, and laughs?
STEVE: I don't know, what?
HARRY: A herring!
STEVE: A herring doesn't hang on a wall.
HARRY: So hang it up on the wall.
STEVE: But a herring isn't green.
HARRY: So paint it green.
STEVE: But a herring isn't wet.
HARRY: Hey after you've just painted it, it'll be wet.
STEVE: But what about the laughing? A herring doesn't laugh.
HARRY: I know. I just threw that in there to make it funny.

ITTY BITTY BEASTS

What was the turtle doing on the highway.
About a 100 feet an hour.

What do you get if you pour hot water down a rabbit hole?
Hot cross bunnies.

How do you catch a squirrel?
Climb a tree and act like a nut.

How do you irritate an oyster?
A noisy noise annoys an oyster.

Why did the frog complain when he got his soup?
There was no fly in it.

Bugs

How do you mount a butterfly?
The same way you'd mount a horse, if you could get one big enough.

How do you avoid illnesses caused by biting insects?
Don't bite them.

What lies down a hundred feet in the air?
A centipede.

Why did the germ cross the microscope?
To get to the other slide.

How can you tell which end of the worm is the head?
Tickle his middle and watch where he smiles.

What do you call two spiders who get married?
Newly webs.

SPELLING

What comes after *O*?
  Yeah!

What comes after *G*?
  Whiz!

First I got tonsillitis, then pneumonia, then hypo-glycemia, and next they gave me inoculations.
  Wow, you must have been sick.
I was. I never thought I'd make it through that spelling bee.

HISTORY

Why did General Custer always sleep on the third floor of his house?
Because that's where his bed was.

What was George Washington known as?
George.

What did Michelangelo say when he was asked to paint the Sistine Chapel?
What color do you want it?

Who invented the first airplane that didn't fly?
The Wrong Brothers.

Why did they bury George Washington at Valley Forge?
Because he was dead.

Why did the two history majors get together?
They wanted to talk over old times.

Where was the Queen of England crowned?
On the head.

What did Julius Caesar say when he was stabbed by Brutus?
Ouch!

THE DAD: When George Washington was your age he was already in sixth grade.
THE LAD: When he was your age he was President.

What did Paul Revere say after his famous Midnight Ride?

Whooaaa!

Why did Robin Hood only steal from the rich?

Because the poor didn't have any money.

Noah and Archimedes Are All Wet

What was the difference between Noah's Ark and Joan of Arc?

One was made of wood and the other was Maid of Orleans.

Which animals didn't come onto Noah's ark in pairs?

The worms. They came in apples.

Why didn't they play cards on Noah's ark?

Because Noah was always standing on the deck.

Which animals went on board Noah's ark?

The lucky ones.

Why didn't George Washington's father punish him after he confessed to cutting down the cherry tree?

Because he still had the axe in his hand.

If George Washington were alive today what would he be famous for?

Being the oldest man alive.

Where was the Declaration of Independence signed?

At the bottom.

When Archimedes leapt from the bath shouting
"Eureka! I found it!" what was he referring to?
The soap.

What was Homer's great epic, *The Iliad*, about?
Sick people.

And what was Homer's most famous poem?
The oddity.

What did they do at the Boston Tea Party?
I don't know. I wasn't invited.

Why did Buffalo Bill go bareback riding?
All his shirts were dirty.

MATH

TEACHER: If you put your hand in one pocket and take out $32 and you put your hand in the other pocket and take out $48, what would you have?
HARRY: Someone else's pants.

If you have six oranges in one hand and eight oranges in the other, what do you have?
Big hands!

If you have two apples, four bananas, two peaches, and one pear, what would you have?
A stomachache.

If two's company and three's a crowd, what's four and five?
Nine.

TEACHER: If a farmer had eight sheep in his field and three ran away, how many would be left?

HARRY: None.

TEACHER: I can see you don't know your math.

HARRY: And I can see you don't know your sheep.

TEACHER: If you had a quarter and lent me fifteen cents, what would you have left?

HARRY: A quarter.

TEACHER: I don't think you get my meaning.

HARRY: And I don't think you get my quarter.

TEACHER: How many make a dozen?

HARRY: Twelve.

TEACHER: And how many make a million?

HARRY: Very few make a million.

TEACHER: If you multiplied 365 and 423 and then divided by the square root of 64, what would you get?

HARRY: The wrong answer.

What did the zero say to the eight?
Nice belt!

How many seconds are in a year?
Twelve. January second, February second, March second. . .

HARRY'S DAD: If I made $300 and gave you half, what
would you have?

HARRY: Heart failure!

TEACHER: If a cord of wood is selling for $100 and you
give the woodman $200, how many cords would
he deliver?

HARRY: One and half.

TEACHER: That's not right.

HARRY: I know, but most of them do it that way,
anyway.

What's a triangle?
A circle with three points.

I'm having trouble with gazintas.
What are gazintas?
4 gazinta 8; 3 gazinta 6. . .

DINGLEDANGLE: If there are fifty states in the union,
and superheated steam equals the distance from
Bombay to Paris, how old am I?
SUSIE: Eighty.
DINGLEDANGLE: That's right. How did you arrive at
that figure?
SUSIE: Because I know someone who's forty, and he's
only half as nuts.

How many jellybeans can you put in an empty one
gallon jar?
One. After that it's not empty anymore.

If a mother and a father have a baby, how many are in
the family?
Two, and carry the one.

HARRY: I got a hundred in the last marking period.
STEVE: Not bad.
HARRY: Yep. A forty in spelling and a sixty in math.

SCIENCE AND SPACE

What's the planet next to Mars?
  Pa's!

How was the new restaurant that just opened on the moon?
  Great food, but no atmosphere.

Why don't they let teenagers become astronauts?
  Because they'd honk the horn, squeal the tires, and play the radio too loud.

What was the largest planet before Jupiter was discovered?
  It was still Jupiter.

Why was the student kicked out of science class?
  He was caught cheating. He was counting his ribs during a biology exam.

SCIENCE TEACHER: Before you start your science project, you have to bring in a card table. For the projects, you can choose any subject. For instance, you might want to answer the question: "Is the force of adhesion between glue and wood greater than the force in wood?" Or perhaps you'll want to show how gears can be used to change the direction of a force. Are there any questions?

HARRY: I have one.

SCIENCE TEACHER: Yes?

HARRY: What's a card table?

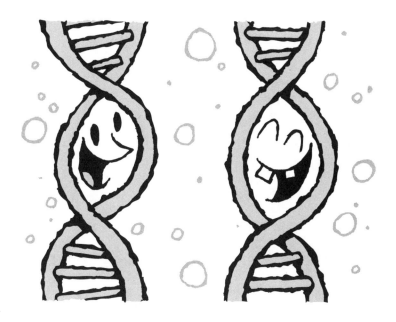

What did one DNA molecule say to the other?
Do these genes make me look fat?

Why didn't the airline passengers want the pilot to go faster than the speed of sound?
They wanted to talk.

What did the astronaut see in his pan?
An unidentified frying object.

THE OCEAN

A freighter carrying ten thousand yo-yo's from the east hit an iceberg.

Really? Did it sink with all those yo-yo's?

Did it sink? It sank 150 times.

What kind of coffee was served on the Titanic?

Sanka.

What's an island?

It's a hole in the water that's dry.

What doesn't get wetter no matter how much it rains?
The ocean.

What did the dirt say when he hit the flood?
If this keeps up, my name is mud.

Why do they use knots instead of miles on the ocean?
Because they've got to have the ocean tide.

What do you do if your boat leaks?
Put a pan under it and go back to bed.

FIRST MATE: (looking out over the ocean) Look how much water there is.
SECOND MATE: And that's just the top of it!

LANDLUBBER: Do boats like this sink very often?
CAPTAIN: Usually only once.

What does the ocean say when it sees the shore?
Nothing. It just waves.

What shakes at the bottom of the ocean?
A nervous wreck.

GEOGRAPHY

What's the capital of Montana?
The letter M.

What do you call a girl guide in Belgium?
A Brussels scout.

My great-grandfather fought with Ulysses S. Grant; my grandfather fought with the British; and my father fought with the Americans.

Gee, your family can't get along with anyone.

Can you name the capital of every state in the U.S. in less than ten seconds?

Washington, D.C.

What's better than playing "The Star Spangled Banner" for hours?

Playing "The Stars and Stripes Forever."

TEACH: How do you spell "Mississippi?"
STU: The river or the state?
TEACH: The river.
STU: M-i-i-i-i-s-s-s-s-s-i-i-i-i-p-p-p-p-p-p-i-i-i-i-i-i-i.
TEACH: That sure is a long word.
STU: Well, it's a long river.

TED: Where were you born?
FRED: In California.
TED: What part?
FRED: All of me.

I dropped my watch in the Hudson River last year and it's still running.
The watch?
No, the Hudson.

What can travel around the world and still stay in one corner?
A postage stamp.

When was the first time you saw the light of day?
Oh, about seven years ago.
You're older than that.
I know, but before that we lived in Manhattan.

What do italics mean?
That's what Italians write in.

MUSIC

What kind of bones are in an orchestra?
The trombones.

What kind of pets are in an orchestra?
Trumpets.

What kind of bows are in an orchestra?
Oboes.

What kind of tube is in an orchestra?
A tuba.

How do you clean a tuba?
With a tuba toothpaste.

What kind of phone is in an orchestra?
The saxophone!

Why did they laugh when the pianist sat down to play?
There was no piano stool.

Why did the musician feel lucky when he swallowed his harmonica?
Because he didn't play piano.

What kind of nets are in an orchestra?
The clarinets.

TRAVELER: I'm so sorry I didn't bring the piano with me to the airport.

AIRLINE CLERK: How come?

TRAVELER: Because I left the plane tickets on it.

OH, I'M SICK!

"Doctor, my husband thinks he's a refrigerator."
  "Why is that a problem?"
"He sleeps with his mouth open, and the light keeps me up all night."

FRANK: I keep seeing spots in front of my eyes.
HANK: Have you seen a doctor?
FRANK: No just spots.

DOCTOR: Could you point your head over there and stick out your tongue, please.
PATIENT: Is something wrong with my throat?
DOCTOR: No, I'm mad at my nurse.

"Doctor, I think I'm a spoon."
   "Don't stir."

"Doctor, I think I'm a deck of cards."
   "I'll deal with you later."

"Doctor, I think I'm a bridge."
   "What's come over you?"
"Two trucks, a cab, and five cars."

"Doctor, my whole left side is numb!"
   "You're all right now."

An invisible man rushes into the doctor's office.
What does the doctor say?
   "I can't see you now!"

"Doctor, I'm shrinking!"
   "You'll have to be a little patient."

A guy rushes into a doctor's office. He has a celery
stalk in his ear, a Brussels sprout in his nose, and a
cherry tomato in his eye. What does the doctor say?
   "You're not eating right."

"Doctor, I just swallowed 20 pounds of sausage."
   "That's a lot of baloney."

"Doc, I think I'm a moth."
   "So why are you coming to me?"
"I saw the light in your window."

"Doctor, What should I do? My son's swallowed a bullet!"

"Well, for one thing, don't point him at me."

What kind of doctor is in an orchestra?
The condoctor.

SUE: My doctor took out my appendix yesterday.
LOU: Does it still hurt?
SUE: How do I know? He kept it.

DOCTOR: This operation will cost you $50,000.
PATIENT: I can't afford that.
DOCTOR: Okay. Give me $9.95 and I'll touch up the
X rays.

Why'd the boy run away from the dentist's office?
The front door said "Pull."

When your head is hot, your feet are cold, and you
see spots in front of your eyes, what do you have?
A polka-dot sock on your head.

HARRY: Last Christmas I got a backache, a pain in the
neck, and a twisted ankle from hanging up my
stocking.
STEVE: How did that happen?
HARRY: I forgot to take it off.

Why does a blonde nurse always carry a red pen?
To draw blood.

"Doc, am I gonna die?"
"Don't worry, that's the last thing you'll do."

Why'd the cookie see the doctor?
He felt crumby.

ANSWERS FIRST

These are answers to riddles. You have to supply the questions.

ANSWER: Apollo 13 and Pathfinder 2.
QUESTION: What was the final score in the Apollo-
Pathfinder game?

ANSWER: George Washington slept here.
QUESTION: What are those cherry pits doing in my
bed?

ANSWER: In the can-can.
QUESTION: Where do you put the garbage-garbage?

ANSWER: Buffalo Bill.

QUESTION: When you buy a buffalo what do you get at the first of the month?

ANSWER: Go west.

QUESTION: What do wabbits do when they get tired of wunning awound?

ANSWER: A pistol, a clarinet, a thruway, and a carrot.

QUESTION: Name a rod, a reed, a road, and a root.

ANSWER: V-1

QUESTION: How did vee make out in the volleyball game?

ANSWER: Freshman Sophomore Junior.

QUESTION: What did Freshman Sophomore Senior name his son?

ANSWER: A birddog.

QUESTION: What do you get when you cross an eagle with a beagle?

ANSWER: Washington Irving.

QUESTION: Who was the first president, Melvin?

ANSWER: A code.

QUESTION: Do you have the flu or a cold?

ANSWER: Sesame.

QUESTION: Says who?

ANSWER: Either or.

QUESTION: Which paddle should I use to steer this boat?

ANSWER: Vitamin.

QUESTION: What do you do when your friends are at your door?

ANSWER: 9W.

QUESTION: Do you spell your name with a *V*, Mr. Vagner?

ANSWER: An almond leg.

QUESTION: How much is that going to cost me?

ANSWER: Evil.

QUESTION: Vill you help me or vill he?

ANSWER: A buccaneer.

QUESTION: How much are those earrings?

ANSWER: Coincide.

QUESTION: What does your mother tell you to do when it starts raining?

ANSWER: Tutu.

QUESTION: How long are you going to work this afternoon?

41

COULD HAVE FOOD ME!

What do you do with a hundred bushels of peaches?
You eat what you can and can what you can't.

Name five things that contain milk.
Butter, cheese, ice cream, and two cows.

What would you call it if a health spa opened up next to the Getty Art Museum in Los Angeles?
Spaghetti.

What does half a pizza look like?
The other half.

TEACH: Use the word "knockwurst" in a sentence.
STU: A light bulb joke is bad, an elephant joke is
worse, but I'd rate a knock-knockwurst.

What do they call lemons in England?
Lemons.

When do you need tomato paste?
When you break a tomato.

What was the weather forecast from Mexico?
Chili today, hot tamale.

What did the girl say when she stopped eating her
alphabet soup?
I couldn't eat another syllable.

When can you knock over a full glass and not spill
any water?
When it's full of milk.

What's yellow and white and gets eaten at a hundred
miles an hour?
A train conductor's egg salad sandwich.

What stays hot in the refrigerator?
Mustard.

STEVE: That sponge cake you made tasted really
tough.
HARRY: I don't know why, I used a fresh sponge.

STEVE: Could you say something soft and sweet to me?
HARRY: Custard pie.

I remember last time you cooked me chicken it really tickled my palate.
You liked it?
No. You didn't take the feathers off.

I'm color blind. Yellow looks like brown, brown looks like green, and green looks like yellow. My friend was eating a hot dog. So, being pretty smart, I went up to him and asked how the cucumber was. And he said, "I'm not eating a cucumber, this is a banana."

If a woman working in a candy store wears a number six shoe, is five feet four inches tall, and has blue eyes and blonde hair, what does she weigh?
Candy.

Do you like raisin bread?
I don't know. I never raised any.

Which side is your bread buttered on?
What difference does it make? I eat both sides.

Where do you get eggs from?
Eggplants.

Where do you get milk from?
Milkweed.

Mom, can I have another apple?
  Absolutely not. Do you think they grow on trees?

HARRY: I know a baby who's only three months old.
  She drinks elephant's milk every day and weighs
  over 95 pounds.
STEVE: A three-month-old baby weighs 95 pounds?
HARRY: Yes, a three-month-old baby. . . elephant.

Why did France send us a two-year supply of hot
dogs?
  It owed us a million francs.

This soup tastes funny.
  Then why aren't you laughing?

Bring me something to eat and make it snappy.
  How about an alligator sandwich?

Why are people vegetables?
Because they're human beans.

I think I just swallowed a bone.
Are you choking?
No, I'm serious.

What's long and skinny and round and fat?
Spaghetti and meatballs.

Why did the banana go out with the prune?
He couldn't find a date.

What did the teddy bear say when he was offered dessert?
No, thanks, I'm stuffed.

What's orange and sounds like a parrot?
  A carrot.

DUCHESS OF SHREWSBURY: What hand do you stir your
  tea with, young man?
LITTLE LORD FAUNTELBEANS: My right hand, ma'am.
DUCHESS OF SHREWSBURY: That's funny, I use a spoon.

Every time I drink tea I get a sharp pain in my eye.
  Have you tried taking the spoon out of the cup?

Daddy, can I have a dollar for the man I hear crying
outside?
  Sure. What is he crying?
"Ice cream, ice cream!"

Why do people near the North Pole eat whale meat
and blubber?
  You'd blubber too, if you had to eat whale meat.

I HAD A DREAM LAST NIGHT

I had a dream last night I was eating a 40-pound
marshmallow. When I woke up my pillow was gone.

I had a dream last night I was eating shredded wheat.
When I woke up a corner of my mattress was gone.

KNOCK-KNOCK...

Knock-knock.
> *Who's there?*

Acid.
> *Acid who?*

Acid down and be quiet.

Knock-knock.
> *Who's there?*

Alex.
> *Alex who?*

Alex the questions around here.

Knock-knock.
Who's there?
Anita.
Anita who?
Anita get into the room.
Open the door.

Knock-knock.
Who's there?
Amos.
Amos who?
A mosquito bit me.

Knock-knock.
Who's there?
Andy.
Andy who?
Andy bit me again.

Knock-knock.
Who's there?
Barbra.
Barbra who?
"Barbra, black sheep,
have you any wool?"

Knock-knock.
Who's there?
Bertha.
Bertha who?
Bertha day greetings to you.

Knock-knock.
Who's there?
Datsun.
Datsun who?
Datsun old joke.

Knock-knock.
Who's there?
Dawn.
Dawn who?
Dawn do anything I wouldn't do.

50

Knock-knock.
Who's there?
Don Juan.
Don Juan who?
Don Juan to go to school today.

Knock-knock.
Who's there?
Eddie.
Eddie who?
Eddie body home?

Knock-knock.
Who's there?
Dummy.
Dummy who?
Dummy a favor and get lost.

Knock-knock.
Who's there?
Ether.
Ether who?
Ether bunny.

Knock-knock.
    Who's there?
John.
    John who?
John the navy.

Knock-knock.
    Who's there?
Little old lady.
    Little old lady who?
I didn't know you could yodel.

    Knock-knock.
        Who's there?
    Luke.
        Luke who?
    Luke before you leap.

Knock-knock.
Who's there?
Nadya.
Nadya who?
Nadya head if you get the joke.

Knock-knock.
Who's there?
Oldest son.
Oldest son who?
Oldest son shines bright on my old Kentucky home.

Knock.
Only one knock? Who's there?
Oprah.
Oprah who?
Oprah tunity. It only knocks once, you know.

Knock-knock.
Who's there?
Oscar.
Oscar who?
Oscar silly question.Get a silly answer.

Knock-knock.
Who's there?
Ping Pong.
Ping Pong who?
Ping Pong, the witch is dead.

Knock-knock.
Who's there?
Tank.
Tank who?
You're welcome.

Knock-knock.
Who's there?
Dimension.
Dimension who?
Dimension it.

Knock-knock.
Who's there?
Plato.
Plato who?
Plato meatballs and spaghetti,
please.

Knock-knock.
Who's there?
Sheila.
Sheila who?
Sheila be comin' 'round the
mountain when she comes.

Knock-knock.
Who's there?
Thumb.
Thumb who?
Thumb like it hot.

Knock-knock.
Who's there?
Tom Sawyer.
Tom Sawyer who?
Tom Sawyer underwear.

Knock-knock.
Who's there?
Arkansas.
Arkansas who?
Arkansas it too!

Knock-knock.
 Who's there?
Wah.
 Wah who!
Ride 'em, cowboy.

    Knock-knock.
     Who's there?
    Walter.
     Walter who?
    Walter wall carpeting.

Knock-knock.
   Who's there?
Sultan.
   Sultan who?
Sultan pepper.

   Knock-knock.
      Who's there?
   Wendy?
      Wendy who?
   Wendy wind blows the
   cradle will rock.

Knock-knock.
   Who's there?
Howard.
   Howard who?
Fine, thanks. Howard you?

   Knock-knock.
      Who's there?
   Picasso.
      Picasso who?
   Picasso of you I'm locked out here.

Knock-knock.
Who's there?
Amarillo.
Amarillo who?
Amarillo fashioned cowboy.

Knock-knock.
Who's there?
Iran.
Iran who?
I rant and rave and still no one
lets me in.

Knock-knock.
Who's there?
Noah.
Noah who?
Noah don't know who's there.

KENYA GIVE ME MORE KNOCK-KNOCKS?

Knock-knock.
Who's there?
Afghanistan.
Afghanistan who?
Afghanistan out here until you let me in!

Knock-knock.
Who's there?
Belize.
Belize who?
Belize open the door.

Knock-knock.
Who's there?
Canada.
Canada who?
Canadoor open please, before I freeze?

Knock-knock.
Who's there?
Guyana.
Guyana who?
Hey, you Guyana open the door or what?

Knock-knock.
Who's there?
Haiti.
Haiti who?
Haiti door is locked and I forgot my key. Open up!

Knock-knock.
Who's there?
Jamaica.
Jamaica who?
Jamaica open the door,
or did she do it herself?

Knock-knock.
Who's there?
Kenya.
Kenya who?
Kenya please open the door?

Knock-knock.
Who's there?
Kuwait.
Kuwait who?
Kuwait a second.
I gotta throw on some clothes.

Knock-knock.
Who's there?
Norway.
Norway who?
Norway I'm going to keep doing
these jokes if you don't let me in.

Knock-knock.
Who's there?
Savannah.
Savannah who?
Savannah, you gonna open the door?

Knock-knock.
Who's there?
Senegal.
Senegal who?
Senegal to open the door if you won't do it.

Knock-knock.
> *Who's there?*
Togo.
> *Togo who?*
Togo open the door wouldn't be so difficult.

> Knock-knock.
>> *Who's there?*
> Uganda.
>> *Uganda who?*
> Uganda open the door or what?

Knock-knock.
> *Who's there?*
U.S.
> *U.S. who?*
U.S. me to let you in. But I don't know who you are.

Knock-knock.
> *Who's there?*
Zaire.
> *Zaire who?*
What's this Zaire? Someone coming to let me in?

Knock-knock.
> *Who's there.*
Israeli.
> *Israeli who?*
Israeli good to see you. Come on in!

GOOFY POEMS

The sausage is a cunning bird
With feathers long and wavy.
It swims about the frying pan
And makes its nest in gravy.

I used to have a girlfriend,
She was six feet tall.
She'd sleep in the kitchen,
But her feet were in the hall.

A boy stood on the burning deck
His feet were full of blisters.
He tore his pants on a rusty nail
And now he wears his sister's.

A cow walked on the railroad track.
A train was coming fast.
The train got off the railroad track
To let the cow go past.

I once knew a girl by the name of Nellie.
She stepped in a mudhole right up to her ankle.
(Wait a second, that doesn't rhyme!)
Well, I'm sorry, the mudhole wasn't deep enough.

Did you ever hear of the refrigerator song?
"Freeze a jolly good fellow, freeze a jolly good fellow."

A peanut sat on a railroad track,
Its heart was all aflutter.
Along came the 5:05,
Oops, peanut butter.

HOME SWEET HOME

What does "unaware" mean?
It's the last thing you take off at night.

How can you tell how long you slept?
Put a ruler in your bed before going to sleep.

What do you sit in, sleep in, and brush your teeth with?
A chair, a bed, and a toothbrush.

Why didn't the kid take the bus home?
Because his parents would have just made him bring it back.

GERALD FITZPATRICK: Last night, my neighbors were stomping on the floor all night.
PATRICK FITZGERALD: Did it wake you up?
GERALD FITZPATRICK: No, luckily I was already up practicing my violin.

I'm thinking of moving to a more expensive house.
Why don't you just ask the landlord to raise the rent?

MOM: Before you come in the house, are your feet dirty?
SUSIE: Yes, but it's all right. I have my shoes on.

What happens when a body is placed in water?
The phone rings.

Do you have holes in your underwear?
No.
No? Then how do you get your feet in?

What gets wet as it dries?
A towel.

What kind of shoes do you make out of bananas?
Slippers.

Why wasn't the man the same after his hat fell out the window.

Because he was wearing it at the time.

Who do you always take your hat off to?

The barber.

What kind of coat do you wear when it rains?

A wet coat.

Why'd Joe fall down with his good pants on?

Because he didn't have time to take them off.

Can you fix this suit so I can wear it out this afternoon?

It's going to take at least a week to wear it out.

If a worker works, how come a finger doesn't fing?

I can swing a pickax like lightning.
  You're that fast?
No, I never strike twice in the same place.

How many people usually work in any one factory?
  About half of them.

Have you ever had stage experience?
  My leg was once in a cast.

This looks like a great play, but it has too many characters.
  That's because you're looking at the telephone book.

HARRY: I'm saving up for a rainy day.
STEVE: How much have you saved so far?
HARRY: Just a closet full of galoshes.

THE GREAT LINGUINE: I'm working on a trick no one else has ever done. I'm going to saw a woman in half.
HIS ASSISTANT: What's so new about that?
THE GREAT LINGUINE: Lengthwise?

Tomorrow morning we're having half a day of work.
  That's nice.
We'll have the other half in the afternoon.

Did you hear about the woman who married four times?

Her first husband was a millionaire; her second was a famous actor; her third was a well known minister; and her fourth husband was an undertaker.

It was one for the money, two for the show, three to get ready, and four to go.

SEE YOU LATER, ALLIGATOR

Why does everyone always say, "See you later, Alligator" or, "In a while, Crocodile? Why don't they say the following?

See you soon, big baboon!

So long, King Kong!

Farewell, clamshell!

Good-bye, fruit fly!

Until we meet again, little red hen!

Adios, little rose!

I bid you adieu, cockatoo!

Good day, blue jay!

Tallyho, pretty doe!

It was swell, gazelle!

Let's embark, aardvark!

Gotta go, buffalo!

Sally forth, workhorth!

Be gone, mastodon!

Vacate, fish bait!

Gotta withdraw, dinosaur!

Goin' away, popinjay!

Heading home, chromosome!

Take flight, little mite!

Take wing, starling!

Make tracks, woolly yaks!

Gotta run, venison!

Disappear, reindeer!

Hitch the saddle, all you cattle!

Onward, big bird!

I'll see you, caribou!

Next time, porcupine!

Ta-ta, tarantula!

Cheerio, black crow!

Bye-bye, mayfly!

Ciao, cow!

Time to shoo, gnu!

Toodle-loo, moo-moo!

Gotta rush, wood thrush!

AUTO-SUGGESTION

What do you call people who sell automobiles?
  Carmen.

I got a ticket for double-parking the other day.
  Where did you park?
On top of another car.

HUBBY: Let's buy a round-trip ticket somewhere.
WIFEY: Where to?
HUBBY: Back here, of course.

MAN: How far is it to the next town?

FARMER: Two miles as the crow flies.

MAN: How far is it if the crow has to walk and carry an empty gasoline can?

CUSTOMER: What's the quickest way to get to Omaha, Nebraska?

GAS STATION ATTENDANT: Are you walking or driving?

CUSTOMER: Driving.

GAS STATION ATTENDANT: That's the quickest way.

How can you avoid getting parking tickets?
Take the windshield wipers off your car.

My father and I drove a horse and buggy.
How did that work out?
Well, my father drove the horse, and I drove him buggy.

COP: Didn't you see the sign that said "Don't Walk!"
HARRY: Sure, but I thought it was an ad for a bus
  company.

HARRY: My car gets a 100 miles per gallon.
STEVE: What kind of fuel do you use?
HARRY: April Fuel!

What's the difference between an orange and a car?
An orange has no doors.

BE A SPORT

It was a boring Sunday afternoon in the jungle, so the elephants challenged the ants to a game of soccer. The game was going well, but the elephants were winning 10 to nothing. The ants finally got possession of the ball.

The ants' star player was kicking the ball toward the elephants' goal when the elephants' left back came lumbering over, stomping on the ant, killing him instantly.

The referee stopped the game. "What do you think you're doing?" he asked. "Do you call that sportsmanship, killing another player?"

"Kill him," the elephant said in surprise. "I didn't mean to kill him. I was just trying to trip him up."

Are you interested in hearing a joke about bowling?
Spare me.

Why did the golfer call his socks "Golfer socks"?
Because he had eighteen holes in them.

How do you hold a bat?
By the tips of its wings.

Daring young man on the flying trapeze: This next acrobatic trick I'm going to do without a net. That's because Annette couldn't make it!

FIRST GOLFER: This is the greatest golf ball ever made. You can't lose it. You hit it into the rough, and it whistles. You hit it into the woods, and a bell goes off. You drive it into the lake, and a big burst of steam goes off six feet into the air.
SECOND GOLFER: Where'd you get it?
FIRST GOLFER: I found it.

NUTTY CONVERSATIONS

HARRY: When you go horseback riding, do you go alone?

STEVE: No, I take a horse.

HARRY: Where do you ride?

STEVE: On top.

HARRY: Do you use spurs?

STEVE: I use one spur. I figure if I can get one side of the horse to go, the other side will follow.

HARRY: Is the horse wild?

STEVE: No, he's very polite. When we come to a fence, he lets me go over first.

HARRY: Maybe you should just ride a car.

STEVE: I would, but there isn't any room for the horse.

You know, you suffer from being a goofball.
Not at all. I enjoy every minute of it.

Just remember, we are born naked, wet, and hungry.
I know. And then things get worse!

I'm looking for a quarter I dropped on the floor.
Where'd you drop it?
Out in the hall.
So then why are you looking in here?
The light's better in here.

I dropped my watch on the floor.
Did it stop?
Of course it did. What did you think, it would go on through?

What's green, grows outside, and has wheels.
I don't know, what?
Grass.
What about the wheels?
I lied about the wheels.

KID: Can I go out and play now?
MOM: With those holes in your shirt?
KID: No. With the boy next door.

Are you laughing with me or at me?
At you.
Gesundheit.

HARRY: My aunt is in the hospital for an operation.

STEVE: What for?

HARRY: Three weeks.

STEVE: I mean, what did they operate for?

HARRY: $2,000.

STEVE: I mean, what did she have?

HARRY: $350.

STEVE: What was her complaint?

HARRY: The bill was too high.

STEVE: Will you just tell me what she was sick of?

HARRY: Operations.

STEVE: Did they at least take her temperature?

HARRY: I didn't know it was missing?

STEVE: How is she feeling now?

HARRY: Up and down.

STEVE: Where does it hurt?

HARRY: Here and there.

STEVE: Is she still complaining?

HARRY: Now and then.

STEVE: What is she complaining about?

HARRY: This and that.

STEVE: Does she complain a lot?

HARRY: On and off.

STEVE: What are they giving her for the pain?

HARRY: Odds and ends.

STEVE: If she's really in the hospital I'm going to go visit and take her flowers.

HARRY: Don't take her flowers. Go buy your own.

STEVE: You should change your shirt. It's dirty. Why don't you put on your tee shirt?

HARRY: It's got tea on it.

STEVE: How about your sweatshirt?

HARRY: It's got sweat on it.

STEVE: How about your dinner jacket?

HARRY: It's got last night's dinner on it.

STEVE: What about your dress shirt?

HARRY: Hey, no one's going to make me wear a dress!

MOM: Watch your language!

KID: English, what's yours?

MOM: I mean, I don't want you using those bad words any more.

KID: But Mom, Shakespeare used them.

MOM: Then I don't want you playing with him anymore.

CREEPY CREATURES

How did Dracula come to America?
He sailed in a blood vessel.

Who did Dracula marry?
The girl necks door.

What would you get if a vampire snowman bit you?
Frostbite.

What did the cops say when they caught a snowman stealing?

Freeze!

What do Alexander the Great and Smokey the Bear have in common?

They both have the same middle name.

What do you call Sir Lancelot with laryngitis?

Silent Knight.

What did Adam say to Eve?

I wear the plants in this family.

Where did Humpty Dumpty leave his hat?

Humpty dumped his hat on the wall.

What's the difference between the Prince of Wales, an ape, and a bald-headed man?

The Prince of Wales is the heir apparent; an ape has a hairy parent; and a bald-headed man has no hair apparent.

What's the difference between Uncle Sam, a rooster, and a bottle of glue?

I don't know, what?

Uncle Sam says, "Yankee doodle doo," and a rooster says, "Cock-a-doodle-do."

What about a bottle of glue?

Hah. That's where you get stuck!

What does it mean to write a story in the first person?

That means to write a story the way Adam would have.

The invisible man got married to the invisible woman. The kids aren't much to look at either.

HARRY

Why did Harry have holes in his forehead?

Because he was learning to eat with a fork.

Why does Harry refuse to eat fried worms?

He likes them boiled.

Why did Harry ask for ten glasses of water last night? Was he thirsty?

No. His room was on fire.

Harry has his mother's ears and his father's nose, and they look pretty funny without them.

Why did Harry play piano for five years, on and off?

He had a slippery piano stool.

ANTS IN YOUR PANTS

Why do people always say, "I have ants in my pants"?
Why don't they ever say they have the following?

Fleas up my sleeves!

Mites in my tights!

A bat in my hat!

Cooties in my booties!

Kippers in my slippers!

A bear in my underwear!

Raccoons in my pantaloons!

Doves in my gloves!

Llamas in my pajamas!

A pig in my wig!

A moth in my cloth!

Kangaroos in my shoes!

A turtle in my girdle!

WITTY AND WACKY

Two antennae got married. The wedding was awful, but the reception was great.

You know what they say, if at first you don't succeed. . . so much for skydiving.

Why pay a dollar for a bookmark? Use the dollar as a bookmark.

Beautify our town dumps. Throw away something pretty.

Louie swallowed ten quarters.
How is he?
No change yet.

Did you hear about the sword swallower who ate a pocketknife?
He was on a diet.

Did you hear about the escape artist?
The guards fed him strawberries, and he broke out.

HARRY: There's nothing I wouldn't do for you.
STEVE: And there's nothing I wouldn't do for you.
HARRY: And that's how we go through life. . . doing
    nothing for each other.

My sister thinks I'm too nosey. At least that's what she keeps scribbling in her diary.

You're the Van Gogh of music.
How so?
No ear.

I was thinking of you at lunch the other day. I was eating alphabet soup and your name came up.

I wouldn't cry like that if I were you.
You can cry any way you want. This is how I do it.

FOUND ON THE AUTHOR'S FLOOR

Why did the millionaire ask for a quarter?
He said the change would do him good.

Why can't you date both Kate and Edith?
Because you can't have your Kate and Edith too.

CHARLEY: I had an argument with my girlfriend, and she came crawling to me on her hands and knees.
CARLY: That's because she was begging you to get out from under the bed, you coward!

How do you keep someone in suspense for twenty-four hours?

I'll tell you tomorrow.

Can you stand on your head?

No, it's too high.

There are ten copycats in a car. One gets out. How many are left?

None.

KID: Gimme a quarter.

GROWN-UP: Aren't you too big to be asking for quarters?

KID: You're right. Gimme a buck.

TEACH: Use the word *"soda"* in a sentence.

STU: You have to bring a lot of soft drinks soda party will last.

MRS. KLOPMAN: Are you ready yet?

MR. KLOPMAN: I told you an hour ago, I'd be ready in a few minutes!

How can you drop an egg three stories without breaking it?

Drop it four stories.

Why is the sky so high?

So birds don't hit their heads.

What did the man in the antiques store say?

What's new?

If the day before New Year's is called New Year's Eve, what's the day after New Year's called?

January 2nd.

Why can't a bike stand up by itself?

It's two-tired.

For every correct answer I'll give you a nickel and a pat on the head.

But I don't want a flat head!

How does love start?

With the letter L.

The following riddle isn't told any longer.
    Why?
Because it's long enough.

What did the bee say to the flower?
    Hey, Bud, when do you open?

What's the easiest way to see your name in lights?
    Change it to "EXIT."

STEVE: Your father's hair would turn gray if he saw
    you like that.
HARRY: No, he'd be happy. He's bald.

STEVE: What would you call the outer part of a tree?
HARRY: I don't know.
STEVE: Bark, Harry, bark.
HARRY: Arf, arf!